Bayerische
Schlösserverwaltung
Bavarian Administration
of State Castles and Palaces

Linderhof

by Peter O. Krückmann

Prestel
Munich · London · New York

Contents

Foreword 7

Linderhof: A Guided Tour 11

   The Residence 14
   The Facades 14

The King's Living Quarters 18
   Vestibule 18
   Staircase 19
   West Tapestry Room (Music Room) 20
   Yellow Cabinet 21
   Audience Chamber 22
   Purple Cabinet 26
   Bedroom 26
   Rose Cabinet (Dressing Room) 30
   Dining Room 30
   Blue Cabinet 33
   East Tapestry Room 33
   Hall of Mirrors 35

The Park 38

   The Grotto of Venus 41
   The Moorish Pavilion 47
   The Moroccan House 51
   Hunding's Hut 54
   The Hermitage of Gurnemanz 55

Stucco on the ceiling of the Audience Chamber

following pages:
Linderhof from the air

Heinrich Breling, Linderhof in the summer and a six-horse ceremonial carriage, 1881, watercolor, Ludwig II Museum, Herrenchiemsee

Foreword

In fairy tales the king is usually a figure personifying everything that is good, wise, and just. Wealth and ostentation are not expressions of affluence and class arrogance but the symbols of inner greatness—symbols that are meant to indicate the grandeur of the king. Important is not that he is a ruler; all that matters is that he has attained the highest stage of human perfection.

Nowadays, when millions of sightseers from all over the world travel to visit the residences of Neuschwanstein, Linderhof, and Herrenchiemsee, all commissioned by King Ludwig II of Bavaria, the question is whether the "fairy-tale king," as he has become known worldwide, is perceived as someone from a distant fantasy world come alive. The only serious difference is perhaps that a literary fairy-tale king lives for his subjects, while King Ludwig, cutting himself off from the world around him, focused only on his own existence.

Ludwig's relationship to real life was, in fact, a broken one. This went as far as his preference for staying awake at night instead of during the daytime. He even regarded himself as the "Night King." The following excerpt from a letter to Richard Wagner is revealing:

> I would also like to withdraw from the dammed twilight of hell that is constantly trying to pull me into its smoky haze. Then I can be happy in the twilight of the gods, in sublime isolation in the mountains, far away from the "day," that detested enemy, far away from the burning glow of the daytime sun! Far away from the profane everyday world, from the foul politics that want to entwine me in their tentacles and would dearly love to totally strangle anything poetic.

In another letter he speaks of the "sanctuary of ideal contemplation" to which he has devoted his life, stating that :

> What annoys me is only the political situation and contact with people that cannot be avoided, and having to deal with the things of this world.

His strategy of retreating into solitude and shifting his relationship to the world into the realms of poetry

O. v. Ruppert, Ludwig II on an excursion in the Graswang valley near Ettal, 1881, watercolor, Ludwig II Museum, Herrenchiemsee

necessarily had to end in an unsolvable conflict between himself, on the one hand, and society, the state, and the constitution, on the other.

One could speculate forever about whether Ludwig would have carried out the functions of his high office with a different sense of responsibility if he had not been only eighteen years of age when he ascended the Bavarian throne in 1884, after the death of his father, Maximilian II. Even if that is what he himself claimed, it is not likely that he would have acted very differently. Throughout what was, after all, a twenty-two-year reign, he was too involved in focusing on the ideals of his dream world.

Another issue that is always brought up is his mental health. Was Ludwig mentally ill or not? The tendency today is to deny that he was. During his lifetime, however, people saw things differently. At least among the ruling class it was clear that this king had forfeited his authority "for health reasons." The end of the story is all too well known. At the instigation of the government, which was in a predicament because of the political situation at the time, and without subjecting the king to an examination, a declaration certifying his apparent mental illness was issued. After it was signed on 8 June 1886, the interdiction procedure was carried out on the following day. An uncle of Ludwig II, Prince Luitpold, took over the regency on 10 June. Finally, on 12 June, Ludwig was taken "into custody" at Neuschwanstein and interned as insane in Berg Castle on Lake Starnberg. The next day the king never returned from his evening walk with the doctor, Dr. von Gudden. How the two could have drowned in the shallow waters along the lakeshore has never been settled.

Thus ended a life that from today's perspective was surrounded by royal splendor but was nevertheless wrought with disappointment and opposition. The latter ranged from the foreignness of Ludwig's parents and his sensitive nature to the radical curtailment of his sovereignty as king as a result of the foundation of the German Reich in 1870, to name only two basic points.

What probably caused most of his inner distress, however, was his homosexual predisposition. Just how much this distress determined his life can be better understood on reading many passages written in his own hand.

The cross in
Lake Starnberg

The Benedictine monastery of Ettal

The construction site of the palace of Linderhof, c. 1868, historic photograph

LINDERHOF: A GUIDED TOUR

Of the three residences built by Ludwig—Neuschwanstein, Linderhof and Herrenchiemsee—Linderhof was where he lived for longer periods of time. He had been familiar with the remote Graswang valley above Oberammergau ever since his youth. He had begun building there at the age of twenty-four. His father had had a rustic "little royal residence" built there as a hunting lodge. The Hochtal valley had a special attraction for Ludwig because of the nearby Benedictine monastery of Ettal, which he saw as a Castle of the Holy Grail founded by Emperor Ludwig the Bavarian in 1330. The striking domed building of the abbey church, parts of which are still Gothic today, seemed to him to support this interpretation.

His wish to build a refuge near Ettal for himself took shape after a visit he made to Versailles in 1867. He found the Petit Trianon, one of the summer residences in the park, particularly appealing. Ludwig XV had it built in 1761–68 for Madame de Pompadour. During the Restoration period, Napoleon III had the main floor restored as a memorial to Queen Marie Antoinette, guillotined during the French Revolution, who had also lived there. Ludwig, who felt he was an intimate soul mate of Marie Antoinette, was therefore inspired

by the Petit, or small, Trianon to build Linderhof. He was less influenced by the outer appearance of its classical architecture than by the intimate and elegant character of the building that is almost hidden in the palace grounds, far from the official life at court.

While Ludwig was still making additions to his father's "little royal residence," the designs for the principal royal residence grew and grew, so that the site in the valley was no longer big enough. He therefore decided, in 1873, to set up his new Versailles on Herrenchiemsee Island. The "royal villa" in the Graswang valley, as Linderhof was called at first, would be expanded into a small palace instead. In 1874, the hunting lodge was moved westwards, where it still stands today. The short period of time up to 1879 saw the completion of Linderhof.

In its one-hundred-and-twenty-four-acre park with four and a half miles of pathways, the king had a Moorish Pavilion and a Moroccan House, as well as a Grotto of Venus, Hunding's Hut, and the Hermitage of Gurnemanz constructed. Many more structures were planned: an Arabian Pavilion and a Baroque palace chapel, copies of the Cuvilliés Theater and the Amalienburg in Munich, as well as a medieval fortress and a Chinese palace of enormous proportions.

King Ludwig employed a whole team of outstanding, competent architects and artists. The basic ideas, however, came from Ludwig himself. The architecture was designed essentially by Georg Dollmann and the interior by Philipp Perron. A group of thirteen artists, whose names are hardly familiar today, worked on painting the interiors. The court garden director, however, should be mentioned by name: Carl von Effner created a veritable jewel of historic garden art at Linderhof.

Anyone approaching Linderhof by car will be on the lookout for the palace in vain. Even when we walk over from the parking lot, it only presents itself once we are right in front of it. Ludwig chose this hidden location deliberately. We will see that this residence

Linderhof from across the park

was intended to have the character of a courtly hermitage, since its the religious background was of great importance to the king.

Throughout the history of architecture there are probably only a few buildings that reflect the personality of their clients, albeit in encoded form, as much as this one does. In the following tour of the residence and the park, with its numerous buildings, we will be tracing these concealed symbolic messages. The numerous furnishings will only be elaborated upon when they relate to these issues. To understand this symbolism is to look into King Ludwig's soul. Pointing out this level of meaning in Ludwig's buildings has been the achievement of the art historians Michael Petzet and Alexander Rauch.

The main facade of Linderhof

The Residence

When standing in front of the residence, the first impression is that of a French villa, though it does have definite aspects of a palace. Because of the sloping terrain, the rusticated lower floor containing the entrance and the servants' and service quarters is relatively high. This is crucial to the overall effect, with the upper floor rising above the massive base in an elegant and subtle language of forms. Even from the outside, it is immediately apparent that behind this facade must be the residence of a king.

right:
The central projection of the main facade

The Facades

The harmonious impression of the main facade derives from its balanced proportions based on the shape of an equilateral triangle. Like a triumphal arch, the

The Residence

central projection rises above three entrance portals. The symbolic subjects of the figural decoration correspond to traditional prototypes. What is unusual is how the thematic program is tailored to suit Ludwig.

The prominently placed goddess of victory, Victoria, in the center of the representative facade, represents the triumph of the Bavarian monarchy,

The Residence

The west facade with fountain

whose glory is announced to all the world by its coat of arms and a crown held by Fama figures (personifications of fame) in the gable. In the entablature below, genii, representing the arts of music, poetry, sculpture, and architecture, stand above the pairs of columns. On the sides of the gable there are personifications of agriculture and trade as well as science and industry.

The foundation of this sovereign power consists of the classes of society depicted in wall niches on either side. Interestingly enough, they are not conceived in the hierarchical class structure of the feudal era. In accordance with the age of the middle class, they are practitioners of the various occupations that keep the state alive: the teaching, military, legal and agricultural professions and trades. The global significance of this structure of the state is symbolized by Atlas the Titan at the top of the gable, the crowning touch of the facade's composition. He carries the entire firmament and the signs of the zodiac on his shoulders.

The other facades are also elaborately designed and are accented by projections whose rounded forms are dictated by the oval rooms behind them. Because of the prosperity in Bavaria, Venus and Apollo made themselves at home here; in their train, wealth, peace, and the arts also settled down. This is the message expressed by the figures on the side facades.

The person who commissioned the design of this earthly paradise is merely hinted at in the back of the building. King Ludwig's showcase bedroom is behind the wall of the central projection. His authority as king derives from the virtues he possesses, which are made visible in figures personifying steadfastness, justice, magnanimity, and fortitude.

Thus, the exterior of the castle is like an open book, which anyone familiar with allegory and mythology can "read." Moreover, in Ludwig's time, the facade's program had an additional meaning in view of the political situation at the time. The planning and construction of Linderhof took place in the 1870s, eventful years for Bavaria and Germany. The German Reich had been founded, causing Bavaria to suffer the loss of essential parts of its state sovereignty, even against the express will of the king. Seen against this background, the decorative program of Linderhof's facades seems like a defiant evocation of former glory.

The Residence

The King's Living Quarters

Vestibule

Statue of Louis XIV in the Vestibule

While the building seems more like a villa on the outside, the inside completely envelops the visitor in the atmosphere of a palace. The passage from the Vestibule through the front room and up the staircase to the living quarters could not have been staged more ingeniously, even in the 18th century.

While the facades' figures and reliefs glorify the Bavarian kingdom, the Vestibule commemorates Louis XIV of France. His statue stands proudly in the middle of the room. It is a copy, on a smaller scale, of a monument erected in Paris in 1699. The reddish marble columns surrounding it like a temple determine the color scheme of the room. The color is meant to be understood symbolically, for Ludwig usually gave rooms devoted to the Sun King a red hue. The columns support the beams and the ceiling above like a baldachin. On the ceiling, the Sun King's head is surrounded by golden beams of light. Two putti fly before them, carrying the motto of the Bourbons in their hands: "Nec pluribus impar" (Not unequal to many). More than merely a vestibule, this first room in the palace was a sanctuary for Louis XIV.

Ludwig II felt related to the French kings in a special way, through the sacrament of baptism. His birthday, the 25th of August, was the feast day of the patron saint of his grandfather, Ludwig I, who was therefore also his godfather. The godfather of Ludwig I was, in turn, Louis XVI of France, who was executed during the French Revolution with his wife, Marie Antoinette. Through this succession of godfathers, the Bavarian monarch felt linked by a sacred bond not only to Louis XV and Louis XIV but also to their forefathers right back to the Middle Ages.

Staircase

After the Vestibule, a rather low anteroom is reached with a matching decorative scheme and a Sèvres porcelain vase standing in its center. Ascending the stairs and reaching the light upper floor where the king's apartments are, should also be understood in symbolic terms. The sunny yellow of the walls covered with marble from the south of France to recall the Sun King changes to a cool, light blue in the ceiling, indicating that these are the living quarters of the Bavarian king. Many more examples of Ludwig's language of symbols,

The Residence

Esther vase, Sèvres porcelain

in which his favorite color, blue, plays an important role, can be found here.

West Tapestry Room (Music Room)

The king's rooms are symmetrically arranged around the staircase. They can be entered only through the two corner rooms at the front of the building, thus creating, despite the compact floor plan, a sequence of ceremonial chambers in the Baroque tradition.

The tour begins in a "Tapestry Room." In reality, the Gobelin tapestries that give the room its name are fake, their large-scale depictions being only painted on rough canvas. The amorous scenes in pastoral idylls are based on paintings by François Boucher and Antoine Watteau. The continuous panorama of images transports the viewer into a remote world of love and harmony—two concepts of major importance in the king's thought. Here in Linderhof, Ludwig had made such an Arcadia come true on Bavarian soil as proclaimed by the bucolic emblems above the lozenge pattern on the wall paneling. Here, where the peace of the Golden Age reigns, the arts, whose patron is of course King Ludwig, are able to flourish. They are symbolized by groups of stucco putti above the doors. The ceiling painting shows the marriage of art and beauty in the figure of Apollo receiving Venus. It is also an allegory of evening, corresponding to the room's west-facing position. The equation of the age of Ludwig II with that of the Sun King is expressly made visible by a Carrara marble sculpture on the

The Residence

mantelpiece whose subject is the apotheosis of Louis XIV of France.

Other furnishings include a life-sized peacock made by the Sèvres porcelain manufacture. It used to be positioned in front of the palace, along with a second one, serving as an Oriental symbol of the monarchy when the king was in residence. A rare Aeolodicon pianino, a harmonium in the shape of an upright piano, is the reason why this room is also known as the Music Room.

Yellow Cabinet

The three following rooms relate to each other in the shape of their floor plans: two, small, semicircular cabinets frame the oval Audience Chamber. The first room is dominated by yellow wall coverings and ornamental panels. Only this cabinet has carved, stuccoed,

West Tapestry Room (Music Room)

and embroidered ornaments in silver. The remaining surfaces are light blue, creating a cool, elegant trio of colors. The delicate depictions in the concavity of the ceiling show allegories of the four parts of the world, the four elements, and the signs of the zodiac. The oval pastels portray prominent personalities at the court of Versailles: Duke Moritz of Saxony, the Marquise de Créqui, the Duke of Belle-Isle, and Duchess Egmont-Pignatelli.

Audience Chamber

The climax of the series of rooms in the west wing is the opulently furnished Audience Chamber, containing numerous emblems of Ludwig II and references to the French court. His preference for rounded floor plans was brought to perfection in the oval shape of this room. Of course, the secluded king never received legations in this relatively small room, which is why the Audience Chamber was also used as an office. This explains the somewhat surprising placement of a table with a gold-plated bronze desk set under the canopy. Besides the gold and white of the wall decoration, the room is dominated by the color green, as the king's offices always were. This leads to the canopy which has a significant two-fold function: it relates to both the throne and to a place to read. This was exactly what Ludwig intended, considering that he did not see himself as an active, reigning king, but strove for the ideal kingship in the manner of Louis XIV. The inspiration to do so came from his insatiable reading. As he writes in a letter:

> ...in the Rococo splendor of my rooms in Linderhof it is my greatest pleasure, which is never exhausted, to delve into the study of fascinating works (mainly of historical content) and to find therein comfort and balm for many a bitter and painful thing that the dismal present, the 19th century that I find so disgusting, brings with it.

The French kings of the Age of Absolutism, through whom Ludwig legitimated his concept of the mon-

Stucco on the ceiling of the Audience Chamber

archy, are present in many ways, primarily in two equestrian statues of Louis XIV and Louis XV on the Italian marble mantelpieces. Significantly, Ludwig chose models for them that had been destroyed during the French Revolution. Another major feature in the room are the paintings in the lunettes, appearing like lookouts on the distant world of the French court. They depict Louis XIV going for a walk in the park at Versailles, Louis XV at an intimate dinner, the reception of a Turkish legation by Louis XIV, and the Dauphin's marriage in the palace chapel of Versailles. Ludwig II greatly valued historical accuracy. The painters often had to make alterations—for instance, if Ludwig thought that the "noble, erect posture of the French rulers" was not shown effectively enough. The pair of small, round tables with malachite tops were a gift to Ludwig II from the Russian Empress Marie Alexandrowna.

following pages: Audience Chamber

Purple Cabinet

The next cabinet, with its purple color, is meant to prepare the way for the adjacent Bedroom. The decorative scheme barely differs from that of the Yellow Cabinet, right down to the portraits in pastels. They depict the following personages: Marie Anne Duchess of Châteauroux, King Louis XV, the Marquise de Pompadour, and Etienne François Duke of Choiseul-Stainville.

Bedroom

In the relatively small building, the king's Bedroom is a surprisingly large room. Moreover, it is filled with the most symbolism and attempts to surpass its model, the state bedroom of the Bavarian prince electors in the Munich Residence, designed by Cuvilliés in 1730. The reason for this splendor can be seen, on the one hand, in analogy to the palace of Versailles, where the bedroom of the Sun King forms the central focus of the enormous building, and, on the other hand, in the complex significance with which Ludwig invested him.

The back of the room is enclosed in a carved balustrade. The magnificence that unfolds here could not be any greater. In the center, under a canopy, stands a gigantic bed, looking almost like a catafalque, in Ludwig's symbolic color blue. Above, in the finest needlework—the embroidery in threads of many different colors gives the impression of a painting—is his coat of arms.

Above the canopy, angels in flight hold the Bavarian crown up in the air. The bed is flanked by two massive candelabras, practically giving it a sacral character. Six fabric panels overloaded with partly three-dimensional, gold embroidery of ornaments and putti make this section of the Bedroom the most expensive part of the whole residence. On the right, a holy water stoop is incorporated into the embroidery; beneath it is Ludwig's praying desk with an image of St George in needlework.

Purple Cabinet

It can be deduced that, in this room, the king wanted to set up more than a place to sleep, for he created an inner sanctum accessible to himself alone, where he sought healing from his despair. Considering that the palace was a kind of shrine closed to curious onlookers, the area around the bed, being completely inaccessible to others, represents a further intensification of the idea of the monarchy. It becomes something sacred and absolute which goes far beyond the significance of, say, the throne. Nothing makes

this clearer than the following diary entry written by the king:

> Holy oath, never to be broken, on New Year's Eve 1873! I swear and vow most solemnly, by the holy pure sign of the royal lilies, within the never to be crossed, invulnerable balustrade that surrounds the royal bed, ...to withstand any challenge most courageously.... To purify myself in this way more and more of all the impurities, which unfortunat-ely adhere to human nature, and thus to make myself ever worthier of the crown that God has granted me. Given in the king's room, inside the sanctified balustrade that is never to be broken into, kneeling on the estrade, my head protected by the canopy over the royal bed. I will neither desist nor err, God help me.

The Residence

Bedroom

This outcry of profound misery, and this pathetic yearning for healing and sanctification also help to explain the ceiling painting of the apotheosis of Louis XIV. Ludwig II could not imagine any other goal in life than complete purification from everything sinful, leading ultimately, after the end of his life on earth, to his being accepted into the circle of the "saints" in heaven. There he was convinced that he would find his beloved French kings again, to whom he paid homage in all the rooms with saints' images. One can imagine that, for Ludwig, sleep had something holy about it, for in this state between life and death he could already feel close to heaven and deliverance.

Once the actual meaning of the bedroom is understood, Linderhof appears as one ecclesiastical building, even as a kind of monastic hermitage dedicated to Louis XIV and XV in which Ludwig II struggles for deliverance in quasi-religious meditation. In another diary entry, he says that to live in the sense of Louis XIV means to overcome evil. His religion is the Christian monarchy, invested directly by God. In its medieval form, this had been the knighthood of the Holy Grail, which Ludwig thought inherent in the nearby Ettal monastery founded by Emperor Ludwig the Bavarian in 1330.

Among the other furnishings, the pictures above the doors are of note. They show scenes from life at the French court: Louis XIV's *levée* (the morning reception when the king gets up), the marriage of the Dauphin in the Hall of Mirrors in Versailles, the *couchée* (the evening reception), and a *carousel* (amusement ride) before Louis XIV in the park of Versailles. Other items deserving mention are the Meissen porcelain brackets and mirrors on the window posts and the mythological figures made of Carrara marble on the tables.

Rose Cabinet

The east wing is identical to the west wing in the arrangement of its rooms. After the Bedroom, therefore, another small horseshoe-shaped room is reached. This one served as the king's dressing room. The fabrics covering the walls and chairs are all in pink. Oval pastels set into the center of the wall panels portray members of the court of Versailles: Beatrice de Choiseul-Stainville, the Countess Jeanne Marie Dubarry, and Caesar Gabriel Duke of Choiseul. Having become familiar with Ludwig's world of ideas, the visitor is fully justified in interpreting these as images of saints.

Dining Room

If one did not know the function of this intimate oval room, one could guess it from the decoration. Carvings on the walls depict the gardening, hunting, fishing and farming that provided the produce for the royal table. These themes are also repeated in stucco on the concavity below the ceiling.

Rose Cabinet (Dressing Room)

This room is famous mainly for its table, known as the "wishing table" after the table that sets itself in the Grimms' fairy tale, "The Wishing Table, the Golden Ass, and the Cudgel-in-the-Sack." By means of a crank mechanism, the table can be lowered downstairs to the kitchen. It is an 18th-century French invention that allowed court society to remain unobserved during their amorous suppers. Ludwig picked up the invention for a different reason. What mattered to the lonely king were not gallantry and erotic adventures but undisturbed reverie when he had his imaginary court society assembled around him.

left: Detail of the ceiling in the Dining Room

Dining Room

Theodor Hierneis, one of the king's cooks, reports on this habit in his memoirs: "He [the king] wants no one around him [at meals]. Nevertheless, the dinners and suppers always have to be large enough to serve at least three or four people. This way, although the king always sits down to eat alone, he does not feel alone after all. He believes himself in the company of Louis XIV and Louis XV and their lady friends, Madame Pompadour and Madame Maintenon. He even greets them now and then and carries on conversations with them as though he really had them as his guests at table."

Two original pieces of tableware are the boat-shaped caskets of gilt bronze which stand on the Tegernsee marble mantelpieces. These so-called *nefs* are decorated with the sun symbol of Louis XIV.

Gilt-bronze *nef* in the Dining Room

Blue Cabinet

The fourth of the small cabinets is hung with blue fabric. The pastels portray Countess Julie de Molly-Nesle, Louis François Armand Duplessis, the Duc de Richelieu (a grand nephew of the famous statesman), Countess Pauline Felicité de Ventimille, and Germaine Chanvelin.

East Tapestry Room

The interior decoration of this room corresponds, down to the last detail, to its counterpart on the west side. The fake tapestries, however, show scenes from Ovid's *Metamorphoses*: Diana and Endymion, Boreas's rape of Orithyia, the triumph of Bacchus, and Europa on a bull. These are stories with which the poet

The Residence

celebrated the Golden Age, when the gods pursued their amorous adventures on earth. Both corner rooms thus revolve around the theme of love, here in classical mythology, there in the 18th century.

Ludwig, who had himself renounced love, here seems to have projected his secret yearning for a time that is distant, transfigured, and hence free of conflict. At least it seems that way, when we view the decorations that he specified himself, which are anything but mere fireworks of beautiful shapes and colors. The ceiling painting in this room, which faces east towards the sunrise, with its representations of Apollo and Aurora symbolizes the morning—by analogy to the West Tapestry Room, whose paintings symbolize the evening.

Chair in the East Tapestry Room

East Tapestry Room: detail of the settee

Hall of Mirrors

Do morning and evening or evening and morning flank the Hall of Mirrors that lies between them? In other words, does the hall stand for the day or the night? Is it the sun or the candlelight that is meant to illuminate it?

There is hardly a spot anywhere along the walls that is not covered by a mirror. The effect of the light is correspondingly fabulous. Like the Bedroom, the model here, too, was a room designed by Cuvilliés in the Munich Residence. Yet the magic-mirror effects have been pushed much further here. Wherever we look, there is a new reflection. It almost seems as though the impossibility of distinguishing between appearance and reality is a symbol of the personality of the king. It is, of course, not a coincidence that Ludwig was especially fond of retiring to a quiet niche here to read. Reading was, after all, his medium for dreaming his way into other worlds and realities. Being a night person, Ludwig probably seldom used this room during the daytime. The effect must have been all the more dazzling when countless candles were burning in the candelabras on the wall and in the Viennese crystal chandelier.

Hall of Mirrors

Everything in this room is very opulent, including the large, continuous mirrors—which it had only just become possible to manufacture at that time—and the centrally heated fireplaces with chimney pieces of lapis lazuli. The furniture, ornamented with rosewood veneer and bronze figures, includes a desk and games tables with inlaid porcelain paintings and a central table with a lapis lazuli, amethyst quartz, and chalce-

The Residence

dony top, with the Bavarian coat of arms in glass mosaic. Also, there is an ostrich down carpet in front of the alcove—an oriental symbol of the monarchy—and Carrara marble sculptures, including a bust of Louis XV on the desk.

Appearing like a patroness above all this pomp and superabundance is Venus, the goddess of beauty, whose birth is the subject of the painting on the ceiling. With reference to Ludwig this means that, thanks to his royal power, Venus was reborn here in Linderhof— and in Herrenchiemsee—an act that can be distinguished on the left of the painting in a view from the lake.

Chimneypiece in the Hall of Mirrors

THE PARK

From the raised terrace in front of the villa, an elaborately designed Baroque-style garden with its pool, terraced gardens, and temple of Venus open up in front of the visitor. This part of the park is framed by hedges and trees, beyond which the landscaped area of the park unfolds. Although the view does not extend far, the visitor has the impression of distance and spaciousness. To achieve this effect, a clever device was resorted to: the center of the valley floor, where the pool is now, was lowered. The jet of the fountain at its center shoots up ninety-eight feet in the air, from a group of figures of Flora and putti, through the pressure created by the natural incline of the terrain.

Behind it, pathways and stairs lead, via several levels, to the upper plateau of the terraced gardens. The symmetry is interrupted only by a three-hundred-year-old lime tree that gave the residence its name. Ludwig, who had an almost religious relationship to certain trees, had a platform put up for himself in its branches which could only be reached by a flight of wooden steps.

A hall opens up in the middle of this terraced garden inspired by Italian Renaissance models. It houses an over life-sized bust of the French Queen Marie Antoinette, who was guillotined during the French Revolution. Ludwig worshipped her like a saint. In an appraisal of the king's mental state is was reported that:

> The Minister, Mr. von Ziegler, mentions that His Majesty always took off his hat in front of a bust of Queen Marie Antoinette, which is on the terrace at Linderhof, and stroked her cheek. And the secretary of the royal stables, Hesselschwerdt, reports that there is a picture in Linderhof before which His Majesty always knelt and before which Hesselschwerdt also had to kneel, his hand raised as though to take an oath, yet without being allowed to look at it.

The "religious cult" of Marie Antoinette practiced by Ludwig, in his own words, went so far that he actually appealed to her in times of need, as though she were a saint:

View of the palace and the Temple of Venus, seen from the Music Pavilion

right:
Flora and putti

> On 16 October [1885], the anniversary of the martyrdom of the sublime and noble Queen Marie Antoinette. May the memory of the martyrdom and of the holy death of the great queen give me the power to overcome evil.

Looking at the garden parterre and the residence from her round temple is Venus, the goddess of beauty. The building is a reduced version of the Temple of Love near the Petit Trianon and thus pays reverence to Marie Antoinette. Originally Ludwig had planned a small theater here, which was probably inspired by the theater that Marie Antoinette had built next to

Bust of Queen Marie Antoinette of France

her little palace. However, it turned out that the site was too small. His idea had been to have private performances, staged only for himself, of plays to be written according to his specifications.

The itinerary through the park continues behind the palace. Here a long cascade flows down over many steps. It is not by chance that a lily-shaped flowerbed of blue flowers was planted right below the king's bedroom. Pergolas on either side lead up the hill to the Music Pavilion, from which there is a view beyond the park to the silhouette of the Ammergau mountains. Beyond the rows of trees and hedges that frame the Baroque surroundings of the palace, lies the

Ferdinand Knab, sketch of the projected theater on Linden hill, 1874, pen and ink with watercolor, Ludwig II Museum, Herrenchiemsee

Temple of Venus

expanse of the landscaped park. Like the royal residence, it is dedicated to the imagination of a king out of touch with the real world. Scattered structures, formerly beyond its limits, mark the stations of his dream journey through distant myths and exotic lands.

The Grotto of Venus

It is just a few steps from the Music Pavilion to the Hörsel Mountain with its legendary Grotto of Venus from the first act of Richard Wagner's *Tannhäuser*. At first glance, the interior seems to have evolved naturally, and yet it is nothing but an artificially created illusion, a three-dimensional stage set. The beginning of construction for this largest and technically most fully developed example of Ludwig's illusionary architecture was in December 1875. The design was based on the Blue Grotto in Capri. To begin with, a pit was dug for

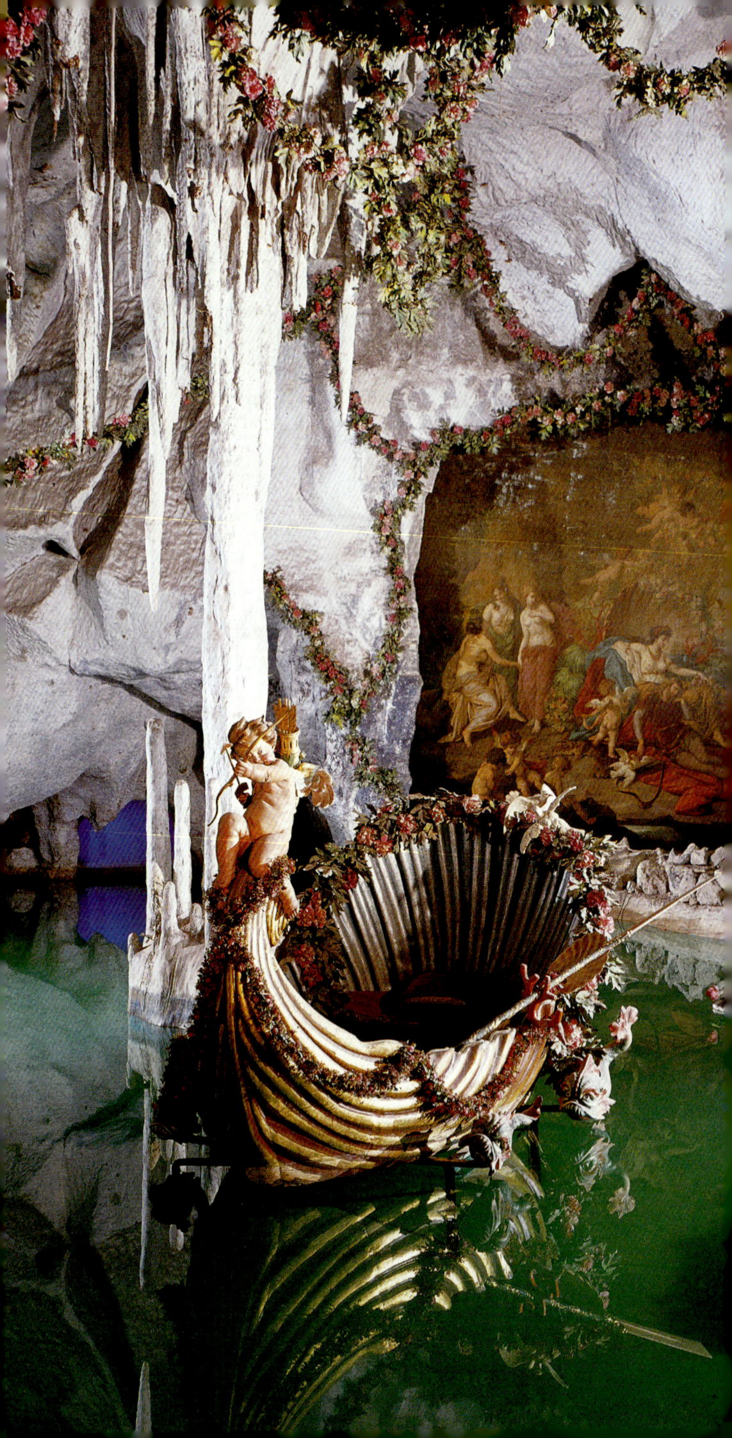

The Park

Music Pavilion

left:
Grotto of Venus

inset:
King Ludwig II in the Grotto of Venus, 1886, illustration by Robert Assmus

43

Performance of *Tannhäuser* in the Grotto of Venus

the artificial lake in the sloping terrain. Then, with the help of pillars, vaulted wall arches, and iron struts, a thirty-three-foot-high space was created. The wall cladding, stalagmites, and stalactites were formed with wire mesh, canvas, and cement and then sprinkled with shiny glass splinters in order to attain a glittering and shimmering effect on the artificial stone.

Through a narrow entrance, an ante-grotto leads to the blue grotto. Most of the space is taken up by the "King's Lake." From a raised "King's Seat," with a shell throne and a table of imitation coral branches, or, even more fairy-tale like, from a golden shell boat, in which Ludwig had himself rowed across the lake, he could absorb the magical atmosphere. The performance in the side grotto behind a stage-like opening, could come alive for him: Tannhäuser, the minnesinger who had strayed from his virtuous path of pure spiritual love, had succumbed to the charms of Lady

The Park

Venus and her playmates. These were basically private performances, such as the king had often watched in the Munich court theater.

Ludwig applied all means at the disposal of the art of illumination to make his fantasy come true and look as dreamily remote as possible. From 1878 on, twenty-four generators made in Paris and Nuremberg were installed, whereby Linderhof possessed the first "power station" in Bavaria. Arc lamps equipped with brightly colored rotating glass disks created psychedelic effects. The king's biggest problem was to find the right shade of blue, and the correspondence with leading scientists at home and abroad was endless. In order that the king could abandon himself to

below: Franz Seitz, preliminary design for the Grotto of Venus, 1875, watercolor, Ludwig II Museum, Herrenchiemsee

Heinrich Breling, *The Grotto of Venus in Blue Light*, 1881, watercolor, Ludwig II Museum, Herrenchiemsee

his dreams during the cold season, many stalagmites were fitted with stoves.

After the numerous references to Ludwig's inner conflicts above, the Grotto of Venus should actually come as a surprise. All his life the king strove for purity and deliverance from physical desires. Particularly in Tannhäuser he saw an exemplary hero. After the minnesinger had succumbed to female sensuality in the Grotto of Venus, he did manage to free himself of it in the end. But it is only in death that he finds his way to the pure love of the Landgravine Elisabeth of Thuringia. Despairing about himself, Ludwig conjured up the singer in his diary: "Tannhäuser, stay with Elisabeth.... only mental love is allowed, but that of the senses is cursed." It is one of the secrets of his unfathomable personality that Ludwig had, of all things, built the cave of Venus, the most lascivious symbol of physical love. It has even been said that he bathed in the grotto with the magical illumination on!

The Moorish Pavilion

Ludwig's fantasies harked back to a wide variety of stylistic elements. These include Islamic art, as in the Moorish Pavilion he had built. Curiously enough, a Berlin architect had constructed it in 1867 as the Prussian contribution to the Paris World's Fair. King Ludwig saw it there and wanted to buy it, but Strousberg, the railway king, beat him to it. It was only after the latter's bankruptcy that he was able to acquire it for Linderhof in 1876–77.

Its iron-and-wood frame is clad in colorfully painted, cast zinc panels on the outside and plaster panels inside. Despite the structure's technical manufacture, its

The Moorish Pavilion

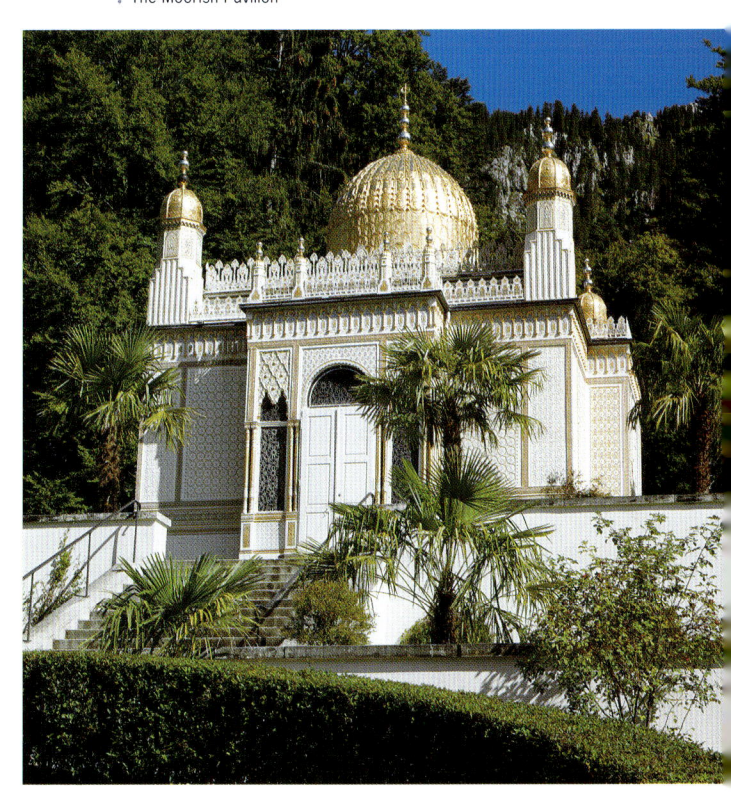

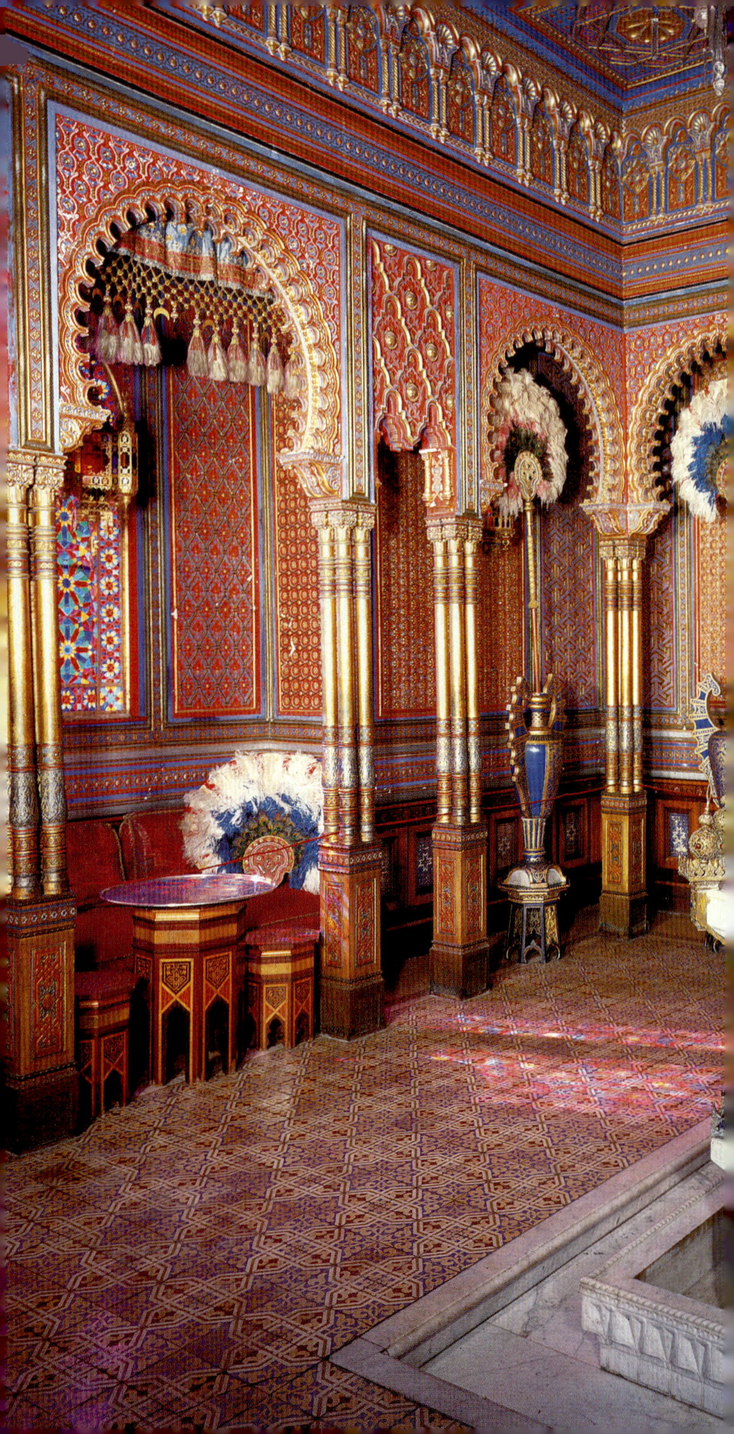

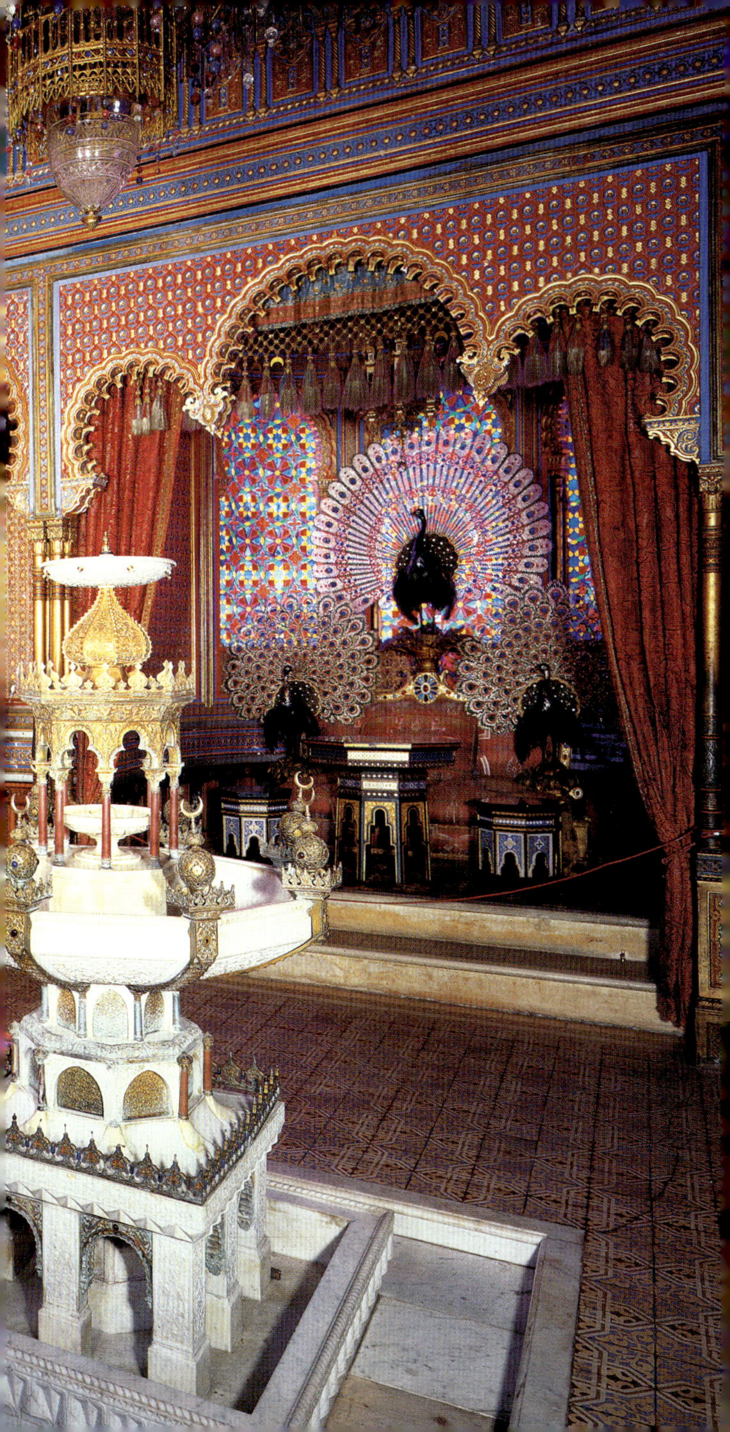

The Park

Heinrich Breling, *View of the Interior of the Moorish Pavilion*, 1881, watercolor, Ludwig II Museum, Herrenchiemsee

preceding pages: The interior of the Moorish Pavilion

inside has a surprisingly exotic atmosphere. Dim light filtering through stained glass into the building creates similarly bewitching effects as in the Grotto of Venus. Electric lamps were installed here, too.

The focus of the interior, which can be seen at a glance from any one spot, is the semicircular apse in the back wall, a later addition by the king. It contains his throne made of enameled cast bronze and Bohemian glass stones—a fantastic recreation of the Persian peacock throne. Like the throne in the palace, it did not serve for official audiences either. Instead, Ludwig could retreat here, letting the room work its magic on him and carry him off to his dream world.

The Moroccan House

The Moorish Pavilion was barely completed when Ludwig commissioned another building in the Islamic style, a palace complex with a courtyard in the manner of the Alhambra in Spain. But this project was too expensive even for Ludwig, and hence he purchased the Moroccan House, a relatively spacious building, at the Paris World's Fair in 1878. When the king had it set up on the alpine pasture of the Stockalpe, numerous changes were made in its decorative elements.

An eye-witness report provides a picture of how Ludwig passed the time here:

> Now and then the king had his personnel lounge around in colorfully embroidered African robes on pillows and carpets, smoking chibouks and nargilehs and slurping sherbet, to conjure up a genuinely Moorish scene.

After the death of Ludwig II the house was sold. It was only in 1980 that the Bavarian Administration of

The Moroccan House

The Park

The Park

The Moroccan House: detail of a wall

left: The Moroccan House: main room

State Castles and Palaces was able to buy it back and restore it. Leaving the park in a westward direction going towards the parking lot, it can be found off the beaten track in the wood above the main pathway.

The Park

Hunding's Hut

Hunding's Hut

At the far eastern end of the park is Hunding's Hut, a reconstruction of the original building which burned down in 1945. The king originally had it constructed in 1876, far from the palace at the foot of the 7,168-foot-high Kreuzspitze mountain. A guidebook dating from the beginning of the last century describes the original location in words that probably capture quite precisely Ludwig's romantic inclination, which led to the hut being built:

> This is probably the grandest part of the landscape of the Ammerwald valley. The wondrous peace of mountain and wood is all around. Splendidly appropriate to the genuine Alpine view of the wide, wild stone bed of the mountain stream is the grandiose aspect of the massive and jagged giant rocks. They tower above the king's idyll, which blends harmoniously into the atmosphere of this landscape scene.

Its appearance is based, down to the last detail, on the description of "Hunding's home" in Richard Wagner's *Valkyrie*. According to this source, the primitive hut in the woods was made of "raw wooden carpentry" built around "the trunk of a mighty ash tree."

Its branches grow up through the "timbered roof." Only days after the king had seen *The Ring of the Nibelung,* at the first Bayreuth Festival in 1876, he commissioned the construction of "Hunding's Hut."

Ludwig often withdrew to Hunding's Hut, as reported by Luise von Kobell:

> Sometimes he sat in there alone for hours, engrossed in reading something, its subject matter the exact opposite of the earthy bearskin ruggedness around him. Or else he enjoyed a tableau provided by the command performance of an old Germanic mead drinking binge.

The Hermitage of Gurnemanz

One year later the king had The Hermitage of Gurnemanz built near Hunding's Hut. This time the source was Wagner's *Parsifal*. It is a log cabin with a roof made of bark. A bell tower in front of the gable makes it look like a hermitage. When Richard Wagner sent the king the overture to *The Ring* in 1880, Ludwig

Heinrich Breling, *View of the Interior of Hunding's Hut*, 1882, watercolor, Wittelsbacher Ausgleichfonds

Heinrich Breling, *The Hermitage of Gurnemanz*, 1881, watercolor, Ludwig II Museum, Herrenchiemsee

wrote a letter to the composer in which he described the place as follows:

> ...in Gurnemanz's lonely cell, which I had built in the woods by the sacred meadow and spring after receiving the delightful composition of *Parsifal* from you several years ago. Here was the right place for it; here one can also see the sacred lake, in which Amfortas seeks to be healed, and here I can imagine hearing the sublime blasts of the trombones sounding from the Castle of the Holy Grail.

Similar to his invocation of Marie Antoinette, Ludwig appeals to Parsifal, who "was anointed with the genuine kingship that is acquired through humility and the destruction of evil in one's inner self, wherein lies true power...O Parsifal, savior...."

After the building had gone to ruin, it was recently rebuilt not far from Hunding's Hut. Nowadays, the picturesque building can only be viewed from outside, the interior furnishings having been lost.

The Park

The Hermitage of Gurnemanz, historic photograph

In these reconstructions of Wagnerian stage sets, Ludwig picked up motifs he had already used to decorate Neuschwanstein, sometimes in murals, sometimes also in a similarly realistic form. Again they revolve around the same background: the king's longing for deliverance. Only the impression they make here in

Ludwigs platform in the old lime tree where he sometimes took his breakfast at dusk

The Park

Landscaped park with view of the Kienjoch

the open countryside is not at all as gloomy and oppressive as there, but fabulous and mysterious.

A steep and winding path leads visitors back to the Temple of Venus, one step from elemental nature back to the Baroque world of symmetry. In front is the palace that can be interpreted in so many different ways: the private home of a nature-loving king obsessed by beauty, or an edifice of ideas transformed into stone, full of the cryptic symbolism devised by an unhappy person for his salvation. The whole meaning of Linderhof is actually revealed only once the fascinating multifaceted nature of the building and the park have been grasped. Perhaps it helps to identify a little with Ludwig's poetic way of seeing, even though the "mystery of Ludwig" will probably never be completely figured out. After all, he wrote to an actress friend of his: "An eternal puzzle is what I want to remain to myself and others."

The fountain in the park

Front cover:
Linderhof, central projection of main facade

Back cover:
The Moroccan House: detail of a wall; the fountain in the park; Audience Chamber

Photographic credits: all pictures are from the archives held at the Bavarian Administration of State Castles, Palaces, Gardens, and Lakes with the exception of pp. 18, 36: Achim Bunz, Munich

Cartography: Anneli Nau, Munich

© content and layout:
Prestel Verlag, Munich · London · New York, 2000

Prestel's 'Compact Guide' series, covering Bavaria's castles, palaces, gardens and lakes, is published in cooperation with the Bavarian Administration of State Castles and Palaces, edited by Peter O. Krückmann

Die Deutsche Bibliothek – CIP Einheitsaufnahme data is available
ISBN 3-7913-2369-5

Prestel Verlag
Mandlstrasse 26, 80802 Munich, Germany
Tel. (089) 38 17 09-0, fax (089) 38 17 09-35;
4 Bloomsbury Place, London WC1A 2QA
Tel. (020) 7323 5004, fax (020) 7636 8004;
175 Fifth Avenue, New York, NY 10010
Tel. (212) 995-2720, fax (212) 995-2733

Prestel books are available worldwide. Please contact your nearest bookseller or write to any of the above addresses for information concerning your local distributor.

Translated from the German by Almuth Seebohm
Edited by Courtenay Smith
Designed and typeset by Norbert Dinkel, Munich
Lithography by ReproLine, Munich
Printed by Peradruck, Gräfelfing
Bound by Attenberger, Munich

Printed in Germany on acid-free paper

ISBN 3-7913-2369-5 (English edidtion)
ISBN 3-7913-2371-7 (German edidtion)